Along the Seashore

Rod Theodorou

First published in Great Britain by Heinemann Library,
Halley Court, Jordan Hill, Oxford OX2 8EJ
a division of Reed Educational and Professional Publishing Ltd.
Heinemann is a registered trademark of Reed Educational & Professional Publishing Ltd.

OXFORD MELBOURNE AUCKLAND
JOHANNESBURG BLANTYRE GABORONE
IBADAN PORTSMOUTH (NH) USA CHICAGO

Designed by AMR

Illustrations by Art Construction and Darrell Warner at Beehive Illustration

Originated by Dot Gradations

Printed by Wing King Tong, in Hong Kong

ISBN 0 431 05562 9 (Hardback)
04 03 02 01 00
10 9 8 7 6 5 4 3 2 1

ISBN 0 431 05567 X (Paperback)
04 03 02 01 00
10 9 8 7 6 5 4 3 2 1

British Library Cataloguing in Publication Data

Theodorou, Rod

Along the seashore. – (Amazing journeys)

1.Seashore ecology – Juvenile literature 2.Seashore – Juvenile literature

I.Title

577.6'99

Acknowledgements

The Publishers would like to thank the following for permission to reproduce photographs:

Bruce Coleman: Dr Eckart Pott p.14, Jan Van de Kam p.10; FLPA: MB Withers p.6; Oxford Scientific Films: Andrew Plimptre p.13, Barrie Watts p.15, Colin Milkins p.25, David Cayless p.27, David Fleetham p.19, David Thompson p.16, p.17, GI Bernard p.15, p.21, p.23, Howard Hall p.23, London Scientific Films p.13, Mark Hambin p.11, Michael Leach p.11, Mike Hill p.26, Paul Kay p.19, p.25, Raj Kamal p.7, Stan Osolinski p.21, Zig Leszczynski p.24.

Cover photograph reproduced with permission of Planet Earth Pictures.

Every effort has been made to contact copyright holders of any material reproduced in this book. Any omissions will be rectified in subsequent printings if notice is given to the Publisher.

For more information about Heinemann Library books, or to order, please telephone +44 (0)1865 888066, or send a fax to +44 (0)1865 314091. You can visit our web site at www.heinemann.co.uk

Contents

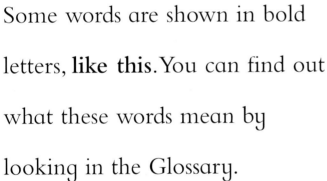

Some words are shown in bold letters, **like this.** You can find out what these words mean by looking in the Glossary.

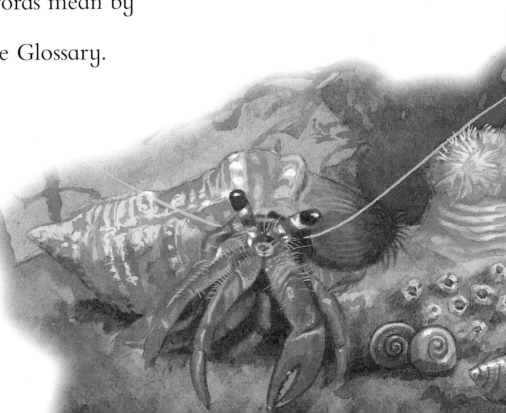

Introduction

You are about to go on an amazing journey. You are going to travel across a beach, and down into the waves. This is a harsh and dangerous world, a battleground between the sea and the land. It is called the seashore or shoreline.

All countries have a shoreline. North America alone has over 160,000 kilometres (96,000 miles) of shoreline, in comparison with Britain, which has 8500 kilometres (5100 miles). As the waves crash against the shoreline cliffs, they break away pieces of rock. These are rolled by the waves on the seabed until they become smooth pebbles. After hundreds of years these wear away to tiny grains of sand. On some shallow parts of the coast the waves dump this sand onto the land to form beaches. We are going to travel across one of these beaches.

All parts of a shoreline are different. Some parts have no beach at all – tall cliffs of rock rise straight out of the sea.

One thing that makes the seashore a hard place to survive is the **tides**. As our Moon circles around the Earth it has a pulling effect on the Earth's seas. This causes the **sea-level** to rise higher and then fall lower each day and each month. This means the waves do not always stop at the same part of the shore. Sometimes they end at the bottom of the beach. This is called a low tide. Sometimes they rise right up and flood the top of the beach. This is called a high tide.

Plants and animals that live on the seashore have to be able to survive the effects of the waves and tides. Sometimes they are covered in foaming cold waves and at other times they are left to dry out and bake in the hot sun. What plants and animals could live in this ever-changing world of hot rock and cold water?

A beach at low tide. We can see the seaweed that usually lives under the water.

Journey map

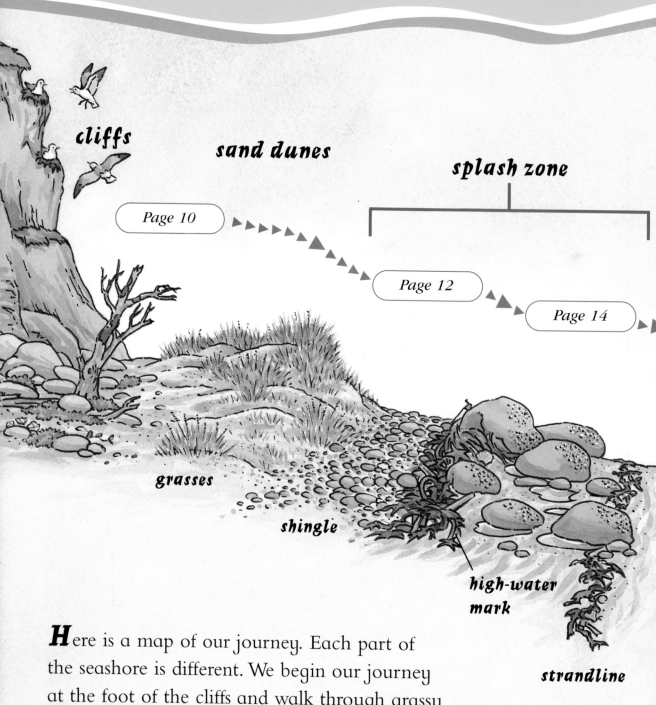

cliffs

sand dunes

splash zone

Page 10

Page 12

Page 14

grasses

shingle

high-water
mark

strandline

Here is a map of our journey. Each part of the seashore is different. We begin our journey at the foot of the cliffs and walk through grassy sand dunes. No water ever reaches this far up the beach, except in very violent storms. The splash zone is a hostile world of baking rock and cold spray

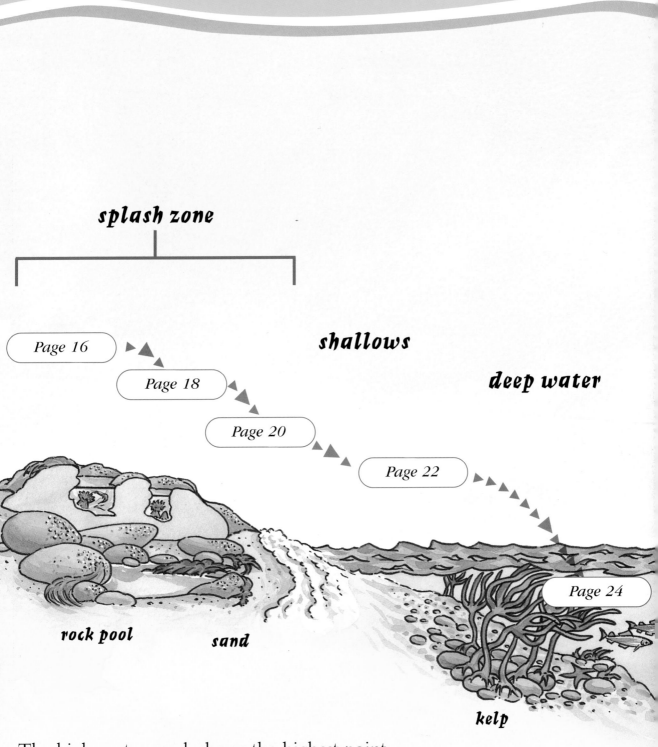

splash zone

shallows

deep water

rock pool

sand

kelp

The high-water mark shows the highest point that the waves usually reach. The **strandline** is where things like dead animals and seaweed are dumped by the **tides**. Then we travel down the beach and into the waves.

Cliffs and dunes

We are standing at the foot of huge cliffs. We can see seabirds flying overhead. Many of them come to the cliffs to lay eggs on the tiny ledges. We walk through the large stones and boulders to the sand dunes. The wind blows the dry sand across the dunes, stinging against our legs. We can taste tiny droplets of salt-water carried by the wind. The sun beats down on our necks. There is no shelter here and not much life. Only tough little plants, like thyme and lavender, can survive this dry, salty desert. They are low-growing to avoid the wind and have tough, thick leaves that store water.

One of the most important plants here is marram grass. It helps form the sand dunes that give a little shelter for other plants and some nesting birds, like this tern.

Kittiwakes

Like many seabirds kittiwakes nest on cliff edges where they are safe from **predators** and near to the sea where they can catch fish.

Marram grass

Marram grass has very deep roots and can spread up to 9m in only a year. Its roots hold the sand in place, stopping it blowing away. Marram grass can form dunes up to 30m high!

Sand dunes

A simple piece of dead seaweed can build a huge sand dune! **1)** As the seaweed rots, sand gathers around it. **2)** If a piece of marram grass takes root there, it holds the tiny sand dune in place. **3)** If the weather is calm the grass will grow and a large dune may be formed.

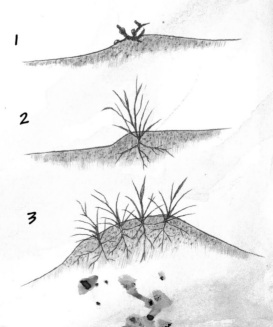

1

2

3

At the strandline

We walk carefully down a path from a high sand dune and jump down onto the shingle. Shingle is made from millions of small pebbles and pieces of shell. Crunching our way across the shingle we reach lines of dead seaweed stretching right across the beach. These are the high-water mark and the **strandline**. Flies buzz over the rotting seaweed. Amongst the seaweed we can see an amazing collection of things dumped here by the high **tide**. We can see dead fish and crabs, broken seashells, driftwood, plastic bags and tubs, and a child's plastic spade. These are all clues to the life that can be found on the beach and beneath the waves.

Many people enjoy **beachcombing**, which means looking for shells and other interesting things along the **strandline**.

1 limpet shell
2 mussel shell
3 barnacle shell
4 oyster shell
5 dog whelk shell
6 razorshell
7 winkle shell
8 topshell
9 scallop shell
10 kelp seaweed
11 cuttlefish bone
12 bladderwrack
13 seaweed
14 sea-urchin skeleton

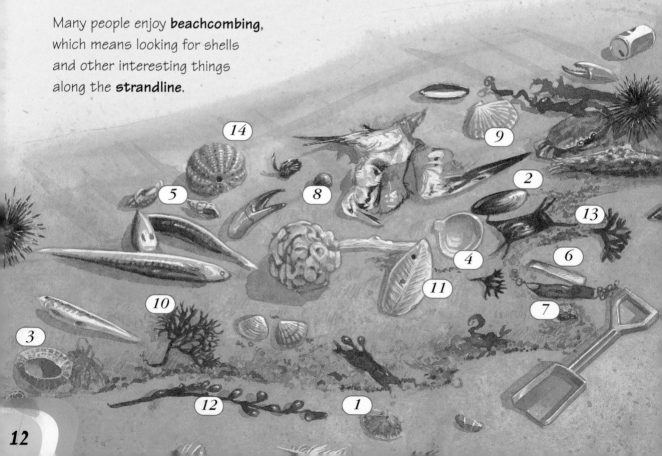

Bladderwrack

This seaweed has 'bubbles' of air growing in its branches that keep it upright underwater. Storms often rip up wrack seaweed and dump it on the beach.

Sandhoppers

If you lift up dead seaweed you will see thousands of tiny creatures hopping around. These sandhoppers like to live under rocks and seaweed and are often eaten by shorebirds.

whelk

whelk egg case

Empty egg cases

Whelks are sea-snails that lay bundles of eggs fixed to stones underwater. The empty cases are often washed onto beaches. Mermaid's purses are the empty egg cases of dogfish.

dogfish

mermaid's purse

The splash zone

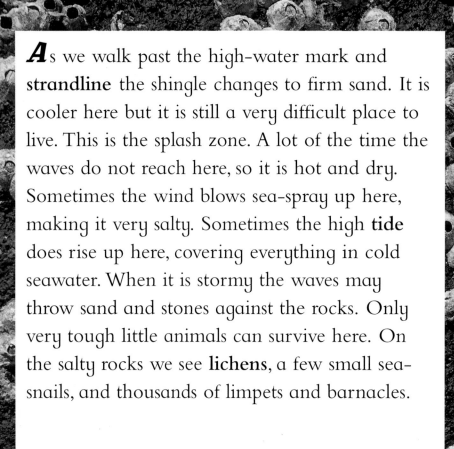

As we walk past the high-water mark and **strandline** the shingle changes to firm sand. It is cooler here but it is still a very difficult place to live. This is the splash zone. A lot of the time the waves do not reach here, so it is hot and dry. Sometimes the wind blows sea-spray up here, making it very salty. Sometimes the high **tide** does rise up here, covering everything in cold seawater. When it is stormy the waves may throw sand and stones against the rocks. Only very tough little animals can survive here. On the salty rocks we see **lichens**, a few small sea-snails, and thousands of limpets and barnacles.

Thousands of barnacles grow in a 'belt' along the splash zone of many shorelines.

Barnacles

These animals live in very tough shells, stuck onto the rocks like concrete. When they are covered with water they open the top of their shells and catch tiny pieces of food with their feathery arms.

Dog whelk

This is a meat-eating snail that attacks and eats barnacles. It has a small **spine** that it uses to open up the barnacle's shell.

Limpets

Each limpet has a strong 'sucker' foot that clamps it tightly onto a rock. If another limpet comes too close to them, they push their shell under the other limpet until it moves away.

Into a rock pool

As we walk down to the lower part of the splash zone we move through some large rocks. Some of them have holes, caves and **basins** that have trapped pools of seawater. These rock pools are a very important home to many shoreline animals. The animals that live here are safe from the hot sun and pounding waves in the rock pools' cool, dark depths. Every day, waves wash into the pool bringing new seawater and food. Rock pools can also be very tough places to live. When it rains the pool may fill up with **freshwater**. When the sun shines the water may **evaporate** and become very hot and salty. Seagulls may come and peck at the animals in the pool, trying to eat them.

Some rock pools are filled with new seawater every day. Others may go for days before the sea reaches them.

Mussels

Thousands of these smooth black **shellfish** grow on rocks across most shorelines. They have tough threads growing out of their base that grip onto the rock.

Anemones

If it is out of the water an anemone looks like a dull blob of jelly stuck on a rock. When the water level rises the anemone opens up its colourful arms. Each of these **tentacles** can sting and catch small **prey**.

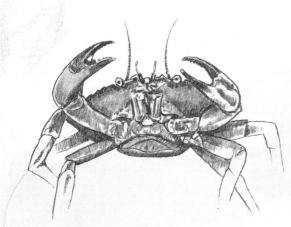

Shore crabs

These tough crabs are like little tanks. They feed on shellfish which they crack open with their strong claws. Be careful if you pick one up – even the smallest claws can give a painful pinch!

A tiny sea

Every rock pool is like a tiny amazing world. Beautiful prawns swim through the colourful gardens of seaweed and anemones. Some of the prawns are **transparent**, making them very hard for **predators** to spot. Tiny fish dart from one hiding place to another, always on the look-out for danger. They hide under stones or in rocky **crevices**. Crabs scuttle along the bottom of the pool snatching up scraps of food. Some animals live all their lives in the rock pool. Others, like the large **edible** crab, are trapped by the **tides** and will escape as soon as the waves return.

1 limpet
2 mussel
3 wrack
4 periwinkle
5 winkle
6 blenny
7 goby
8 anemone
9 velvet swimming crab
10 prawn
11 cushion star
12 hermit crab
13 edible crab

Rock pools are wonderful places to look for seashore life, but do not take any of the creatures away.

Hermit crab

These tiny crabs have no shell of their own. They live in the shells of dead sea-snails. When they grow too big for their shell they quickly crawl out and hop into a bigger new shell.

Goby

This tiny fish has a sucker on its belly to help it grip onto the rocks when the waves wash into the pool. It has bulging eyes on the top of its head to look upwards for predators like seagulls.

Prawn

Prawns walk or swim slowly forwards around the pool. If attacked they pull their tails back suddenly which shoots them backwards away from danger.

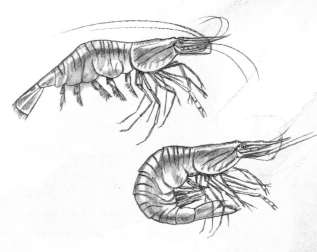

On the beach

We are now moving down the slope of the beach towards the waves. It is cooler and very fresh here. The waves wash up the beach, wetting the sand. We cannot see any animals at all and yet there are thousands all around us – right beneath our feet!

A huge number of worms, sea-snails, starfish and other small animals live buried in the wet sand. Some scrape tiny pieces of food off the sand itself. Others are hiding from **predators**, waiting for the **tide** to rise. When it does, this part of the beach will be underwater for a few hours. The hidden animals come out of their burrows and feed off tiny **particles** of food in the seawater.

1 *oystercatcher*
2 *lugworm*
3 *cockle*
4 *razorshell*
5 *burrowing starfish*
6 *sea-potato*
7 *sea-mouse*

Shorebirds like sanderlings and oystercatchers run up and down the beach hunting for hidden **shellfish** and worms.

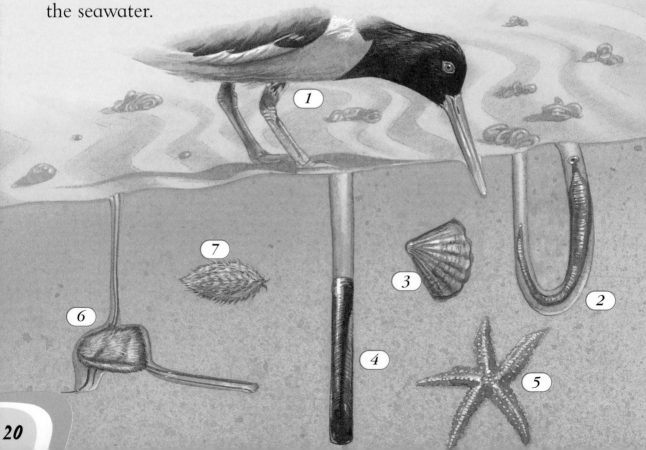

Oystercatcher

These shorebirds look for shellfish that are poking out of the sand with their shells slightly open. The oystercatcher stabs the **muscle** that closes the shells and then opens up the shells and eats the inside.

Lugworm

Thousands of these worms live in U-shaped burrows under the sand. They leave a little mound of sand at the top of their burrow called a **cast**.

Razorshell

The razorshell is named after old cut-throat razors. It burrows into the sand with its muscular foot. Its thin shape helps it to slide down its burrow if attacked by a predator.

Kelp forests

We put on our **masks** and **snorkels** and wade into the chilly water. Small waves slap against us. We take a deep breath and dive into the shallows.

All around us are long, brown, underwater weeds growing from the seabed up towards the light. The weeds wave backwards and forwards as the waves roll in above. This seaweed is called kelp. Each kelp plant has roots called a holdfast, which grip onto the rocks and seabed. It covers the seabed in a long strip, just like a forest. This forest forms an important home for many animals. Sea-urchins and limpets graze on the kelp, just like rabbits and deer. Fish, crabs and starfish are the forest **predators**, moving through the holdfasts looking for food.

Kelp forests protect many animals from the heat of the sun and the force of the waves.

Kelp ——→

Kelp only usually grows in water about 3 m deep, where there is still plenty of sunlight. Giant kelp grows in very warm, bright water. It grows in much deeper water and can reach lengths of up to 30 m long. It can grow up to a metre in just one day!

Sea-urchin

Sea-urchins have tough, sharp jaws under their bodies. They move slowly through the kelp, feeding on its **stipes** and holdfasts. Sharp **spines** protect the urchins from predators.

Dogfish ——→

Dogfish are a small kind of shark. They lay their eggs amongst the kelp. The egg cases have **tendrils** at the ends which wind around the stipes and hold the egg in place (see page 13).

Beyond the shallows

We swim out of the dark, dense kelp forest into deeper water. There is a long stretch of flat sand on the seabed beneath us. We swim down to the sand and glide just above it. We cannot see any signs of life. Suddenly there is a burst of sand in front of us and we see something swim away. We have disturbed a large flatfish, hidden on top of the sand. There are many other creatures hidden here under the sand or amongst the clumps of rocks and weed.

The sun is going down, and the water is getting cold. Many more creatures will come out at night to feed. It is time to end our journey and return to the shore.

Lobsters live in deeper waters hiding in holes amongst the rocks. They come out at night to look for dead fish and other scraps of food.

Turbot

This flatfish can change the colour of its skin to match the colour of the sand and rocks around it. In this way the flatfish stays hidden from **predators** and can gobble up smaller fish that come too close.

Acorn barnacle →

Barnacles live on rocks in huge numbers, like mussels. Sometimes it is hard to find any space left on a rock. Here acorn barnacles have found a different home – on top of a mussel shell!

Piddock

The end of a piddock looks like an oil drill **bit**. Just like a drill, it turns round and round to grind its way through sand, or even rock, to make a burrow.

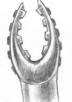

end of piddock shell   oil drill bit

Conservation and the future

The seashore is a wonderful place to visit, but it is also an easy place to damage. Cliff edges and sand dunes are important homes to nesting seabirds. Too many tourists will scare the birds away and may **erode** the cliff edges. Sand dunes are also easily damaged by people. Just one small hole made in the marram grass can allow the wind to whistle through. Soon the hole gets wider and wider until it destroys the dune. Walking over rocks can also crush and kill **shellfish** like barnacles.

Pollution is a much bigger threat. Chemicals and sewage dumped into the water kills fish, seaweeds and shellfish like limpets and mussels. Oil spills can kill thousands of seabirds and ruin beaches for hundreds of miles.

The seashores of northeastern America and the Mediterranean have been badly polluted in the past.

Protecting the seashore

Many countries are now trying to look after their seashores and coastlines. They have stopped sewage dumping near the shore and cleaned oil off their beaches. Some have turned hundreds of miles of coastline into National Parks where the wildlife is protected from pollution and tourism.

You can help protect your seashore. Always use paths and walkways that have been built through sand dunes. Do not take anything alive away from the seashore or a rock pool. If you turn over a rock to look underneath, put it back carefully. Never leave rubbish on the beach. Unless we protect these wonderful places there will be no more amazing journeys to make along the seashore.

These people are clearing up oil on a beach.

Glossary

basins	a dip in the land into which water falls and collects
beachcombing	collecting things that have washed up onto the beach
bit	the cutting part of a drill
cast	the sand thrown up on the surface which has been tunelled out by the worm
crevice	a narrow crack
edible	something you can eat
erode	to wear away
evaporate	when a liquid dries up and becomes either a dry or a gas-like substance
freshwater	fresh river or stream water, not salty seawater
lichen	light green plant that grows on rocks or trees
mask	divers wear masks to protect and keep their eyes dry under the water
muscle	lots of small fibres in a body that help to make it move
particle	a very small amount of something
predator	an animal that hunts, kills and eats other animals
prey	animals that are hunted by predators
sea-level	the height of the sea at different times
shellfish	animal that lives in water and has a hard outer shell, like an oyster or a mussel
snorkel	tube that is held in the mouth and sticks out of the water and helps swimmers to breathe just under water

spines	a special sharp, pointed bone or stiff fish fin
stipes	the stalk part of the kelp seaweed
strandline	the area of the beach where objects are washed up by the high tide
tendril	special leaf or stem that some animals or climbing plants use to fix themselves to something
tentacle	a long and flexible part of some animals that is used to feel or touch
tide	the rise and fall of the surface of the sea at different times
transparent	see-through

Further reading and addresses

Books

Coasts, Keith Lye, Our World series, Wayland, 1987

Hard and Soft, (A look at Crabs and Octopi), Rod Theodorou and Carole Telford, Animal Opposites series, Heinemann Library, 1996

Inside a Coral Reef, Carole Telford and Rod Theodorou, Amazing Journeys series, Heinemann Library, 1997

Seashore, Peter Hayward, Tony Nelson-Smith and Chris Shields, Collins Pocket Guide series, Collins, 1996

Seashore, Steve Parker, Eyewitness Guides series, Dorling Kindersley, 1989

Seas and Oceans, Our World series, David Lambert, Wayland, 1987

Secrets of the Seashore, Derek Hall, The Living Countryside series, Reader's Digest, 1984

The Dying Sea, Survival series, Michael Bright, Aladdin Books, 1988

The Living Seashore, Nature Watch series, Franklin Watts, 1992

To the Depths of the Ocean, Rod Theodorou, Amazing Journeys series, Heinemann Library, 2000

Organizations

Birdlife International, Wellbrook Court, Girton Road, Cambridge, CB3 0NA, UK

British Trust for Conservation Volunteers, 36 St. Mary's Street, Wallingford, Oxford, OX10 0EU, UK

Earthwatch, Belsyre Court, 57 Woodstock Road, Oxford, OX2 6HU, UK

Friends of the Earth, 26-28 Underwood Street, London N1 2PN, UK, Tel (0171) 490 1555

Greenpeace, Canonbury Villas, London, N1 2PN, UK, Tel (0171) 354 5100

Marine Conservation Society, 4 Gloucester Road, Ross-on-Wye, Herefordshire, HR9 5AU, UK

Royal Society for Nature Conservation, The Green, Nettleham, London LN2 2NR, UK

Royal Society for the Protection of Birds, The Lodge, Sandy, Bedfordshire SG19 2DL, UK, Tel (01767) 680551

Waste Watch, National Council for Voluntary Organisations, 26 Bedford Square, London, WC1B 3HU, UK

World Wide Fund for Nature, Panda House, Weyside Park, Catteshall Lane, Godalming, Surrey GU7 1XR, UK, Tel (01483) 426444

Index